W9-BUJ-513

Police Officers/Policías

By Jacqueline Laks Gorman

Reading consultant: Susan Nations, M.Ed., author/literacy coach/consultant

Gareth Stevens
Publishing

Please visit our Web site www.garethstevens.com. For a free color catalog of all our high-quality books, call toll free 1-800-542-2595 or fax 1-877-542-2596.

Cataloging Data

Gorman, Jacqueline Laks, 1955-
    Police officers / Policias by Jacqueline Laks Gorman.
        p. cm. — (People in my community)
    Summary: Explains what police officers do, including helping people
in trouble, stopping people who break the law, and directing traffic. Bilingual Edition
    Includes bibliographical references and index.
    ISBN: 978-1-4339-3769-9 (pbk.)
    ISBN: 978-1-4339-3770-5 (6-pack)
    ISBN: 978-1-4339-3768-2 (library binding)
    1. Police—Juvenile literature. [1. Police. 2. Occupations. 3. Spanish-language materials] I. Title.

New edition published 2010 by
Gareth Stevens Publishing
111 East 14th Street, Suite 349
New York, NY 10003

New text and images this edition copyright © 2010 Gareth Stevens Publishing

Original edition published 2003 by Weekly Reader® Books
An imprint of Gareth Stevens Publishing
Original edition text and images copyright © 2003 Gareth Stevens Publishing

Art direction: Haley Harasymiw, Tammy Gruenewald
Page layout: Michael Flynn, Katherine A. Goedheer
Editorial direction: Kerri O'Donnell, Diane Laska Swanke
Spanish translation: Eduardo Alamán

Photo credits: Cover, back cover, p. 1 © Darrin Klimek/Digital Vision/Getty Images; pp. 5, 15 © Shutterstock.com; pp. 7, 9, 11, 13, 17, 19, 21 by Gregg Andersen.

Printed in the United States of America

CPSIA compliance information: Batch #WW10GS: For further information contact Gareth Stevens, New York, New York at 1-800-542-2595.

Table of Contents

Contenido

Boldface words appear in the glossary/
Las palabras en **negrita** aparecen en el glosario

An Important Job

A police officer has an important job. A police officer helps people.

Un trabajo importante

Los policías tienen un trabajo muy importante. Los policías ayudan a las personas.

A police officer helps people in trouble. A police officer helps keep people safe.

Los policías ayudan a las personas que están en problemas. Los policías nos mantienen seguros.

Police Gear

Police officers wear **badges** and special **uniforms**. They use radios to talk to each other.

El equipo de los policías

Los policías usan **insignias** y **uniformes** especiales. Además, usan radios para comunicarse.

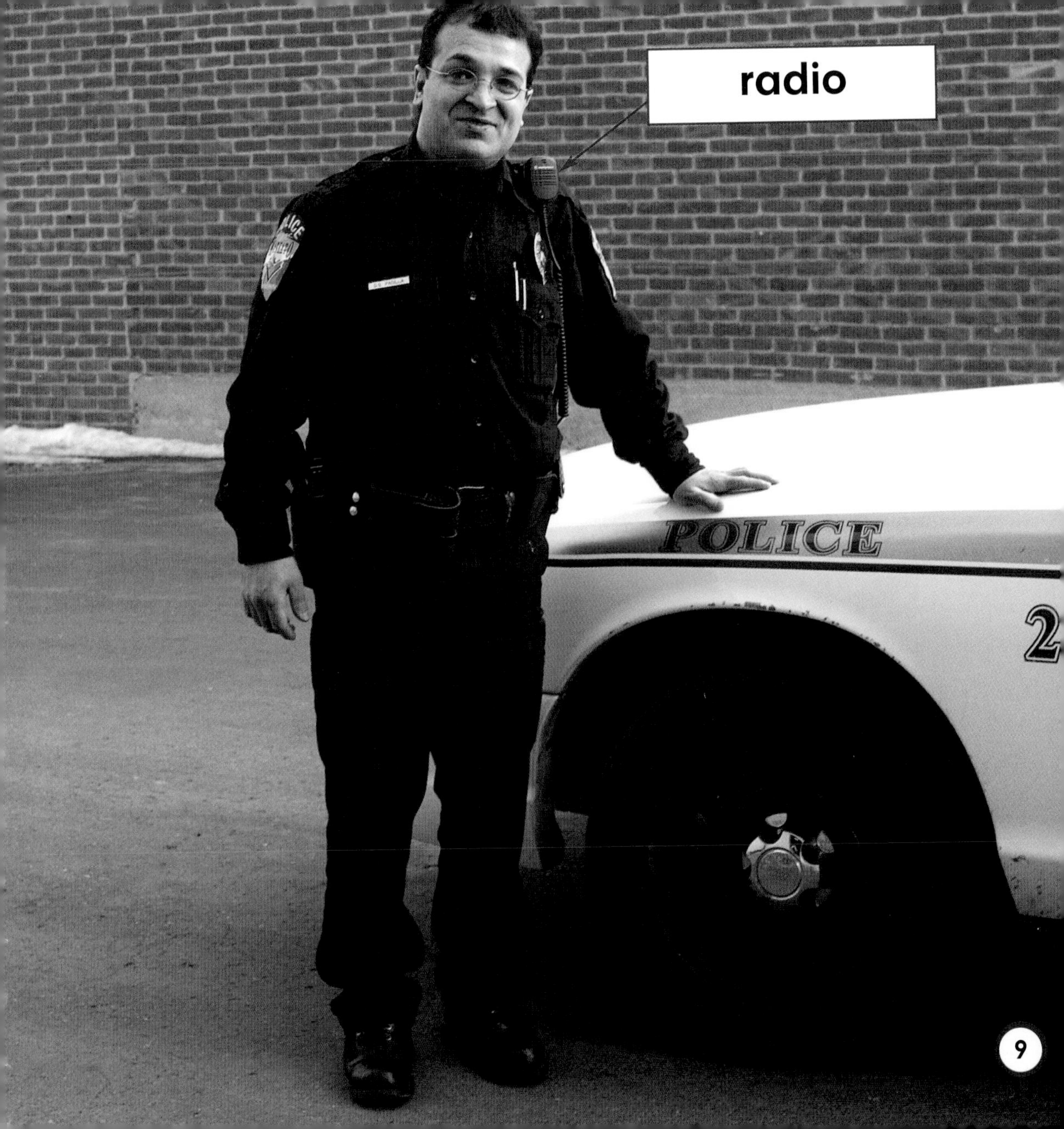
radio
POLICE
2

A Safe Neighborhood

Police officers stop people who break the **law**. They help keep your **neighborhood** safe.

Un barrio seguro

Los policías detienen a las personas que burlan las **leyes**. Los policías mantienen seguros los **barrios**.

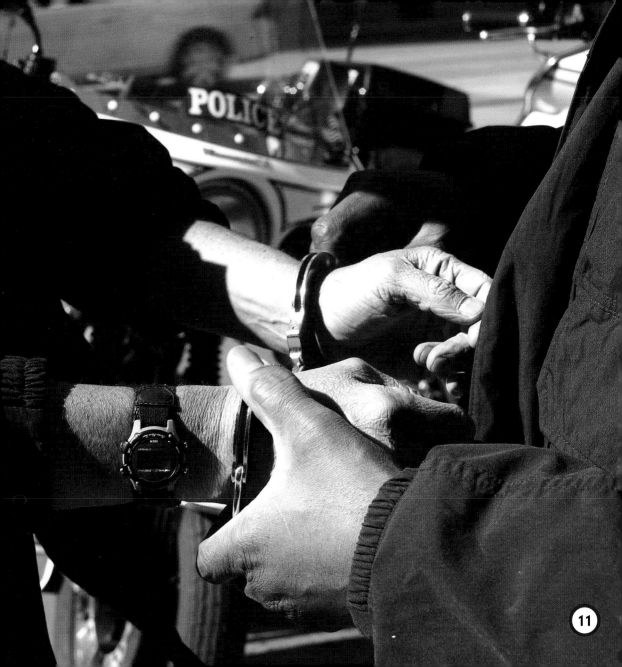

Some police officers ride in police cars. Some ride on motorcycles.

Algunos policías viajan en coches de policía. Otros viajan en motocicletas.

**motorcycles/
motocicletas**

Sometimes police officers direct traffic. They give tickets to drivers who drive too fast.

A veces los policías dirigen el tráfico. Los policías multan a las personas que manejan muy rápido.

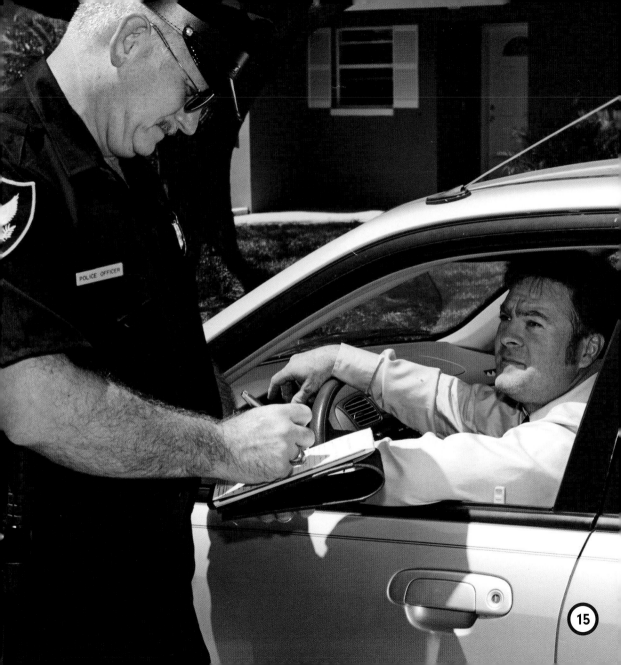

Sometimes police officers visit schools. They talk about how to stay safe.

A veces los policías visitan las escuelas. Los policías nos explican cómo mantenernos seguros.

If you are ever lost or need help, a police officer can help you.

Si algún día te pierdes o necesitas ayuda, puedes llamar a un policía.

Would you like to be a
police officer?

¿Te gustaría ser policía?

Glossary/Glosario

badge: a small sign that identifies people and is pinned to their clothes

law: a rule that people follow

neighborhood: the streets and homes around the place you live

uniform: clothing worn by members of a group such as firefighters, mail carriers, or police officers

- - - - - - - - - - - - - - - - - - -

barrio (el) las calles y casas alrededor de donde vives

insignia (la) un pequeño signo que identifica a las personas. Se usa en la ropa

ley (la) reglas que siguen las personas

uniforme (el) ropa especial que usan los policías, carteros o bomberos

For More Information/Más información

Books/Libros

Leake, Diyan. *La policía.* Coughlan Publishing, 2009

Lindeen, Carol K. *Patrullas de policía / Police Cars.* Capstone Press, 2006

Web Sites/Páginas en Internet

Free Police and Safety Coloring and Activity Pages
http://kids.askacop.org/coloringpages.html

Index/Índice

About the Author

Jacqueline Laks Gorman is a writer and editor. She grew up in New York City and began her career working on encyclopedias and other reference books. Since then, she has worked on many different kinds of books. She lives with her husband and children, Colin and Caitlin, in DeKalb, Illinois.

- -

Información sobre la autora

Jacqueline Laks Gorman es escritora y editora. Jacqueline creció en la ciudad de Nueva York donde comenzó su carrera trabajando en enciclopedias y libros de referencia. Desde entonces ha trabajado en muchos libros infantiles. Jacqueline vive con su esposo y sus hijos, Colin y Caitlin, en DeKalb, Illinois.